Rookie Read-About™ Science

It Could Still Be A Bird

By Allan Fowler

Images supplied by VALAN Photos

Consultants:
Robert L. Hillerich, Ph.D., Bowling Green
State University, Bowling Green, Ohio

Mary Nalbandian, Director of Science,
Chicago Public Schools, Chicago, Illinois

CHILDRENS PRESS®

CHICAGO

Series cover and interior design by Sara Shelton

Library of Congress Cataloging-in-Publication Data

Fowler, Allan.
  It could still be a bird / by Allan Fowler.
    p. cm.—(Rookie read-about science)
    Summary: Identifies the characteristics of birds and provides
  specific examples including the penguin, ostrich, peacock, and
  pelican.
    ISBN 0-516-04901-1
    1. Birds—Juvenile literature. [1. Birds.] I. Title.
  II. Series.
  QL676.2.F68 1990   90-2206
  598—dc20   CIP
                                                       AC

How do you know
it's a bird?

If it has feathers

and wings

and it flies

and it lays eggs,
it's a bird!

But what if it doesn't fly?
It could still be a bird

like a penguin.

What if it's so tiny, it can
stand on your finger?
It could still be a bird

like a hummingbird.

What if it's bigger
than you are?
It could still be a bird

like an ostrich.

A bird could be
as plain as a sparrow

or as fancy as a peacock.

A bird could be
as graceful as a swan

or as funny as a pelican.

A bird could be
as red as a cardinal

or as blue as a jay.

20

A bird can be many
different colors,
like a macaw.

A bird could live
in a tree near your house,

in the woods,

in a farmyard,

or in the zoo.
It's still a bird.

But even if it flies
and even if it lays eggs,
if it
     doesn't have

          FEATHERS,
it's not a bird!

All birds have feathers.

Words You Know

penguin

hummingbird

ostrich

sparrow

peacock

swan

pelican

cardinal

blue jay

macaw

Index

About the Author

Allan Fowler is a free-lance writer with a background in advertising. Born in New York, he lives in Chicago now and enjoys traveling.

Photo Credits

Valan—© Robert C. Simpson, Cover, 18, 23, 29, 31 (center left); © Wayne Lankinen, 4, 5, 11, 19, 30 (top right), 31 (center right); © Harold V. Green, 6; © Michel Quintin, 7; © Fred Bruemmer, 9, 30 top left); © B. Lyon, 13, 30 (center left); © Y. R. Tymstra, 14, 30 (center right); © J. A. Wilkinson, 15, 30 (bottom); © K. Ghani, 16, 31 (top left); © R. Berchin, 17, 31 (top right); © Herman H. Giethoorn, 20, 31 (bottom); © Esther Schmidt, 24; © V. Wilkinson, 25; © Marguerite Servais, 26
COVER: Cardinal